GW00648887

Cara Delevingne, makes us all go green
With envy as we witness the best eyebrows we have seen!

She struts her stuff for Burberry, Gucci, Prada and Preen
The front row sit in awe as she lowers their self esteem

Her face is animated, she's every photographer's dream
Her pout is like a pillow, her smile like a laser beam

Magazines united, one thing they're all agreeing
CARA IS A MEGA GORGEOUS SUPER HUMAN BEING!

Mel
x

Published by
I LOVE MEL
United Kingdom
978-0-9567208
July 2013

I Love Mel is a trading name of Brolly Associates Ltd
www.ilovemel.me mel@ilovemel.me
©M S Elliott 2013

ISBN Number
978-0-9573148-7-0

Distributed in the United States and Canada by SCB Distributors.
Distributed outside of the United States and Canada by Turnaround Publisher Services.